The Really **Wild Life** of **Snakes**™

COTTONMOUTHS

HEATHER FELDMAN

The Rosen Publishing Group's

PowerKids Press™
New York

For Sophie and Matthew, with all my love

Published in 2004 by The Rosen Publishing Group, Inc.
29 East 21st Street, New York, NY 10010

First Edition

Editor: Kathy Kuhtz Campbell
Book Design: Mike Donnellan, Michael de Guzman

Photo Credits: Cover © Gary W. Carter/CORBIS; back cover, pp. 4, 19 © John Cancalosi; pp. 7, 7 (inset), 12, 15, 15 (inset), 20 © Peter May; p. 8 © Raymond Gehman/CORBIS; p. 11 © David A. Northcott/CORBIS; p. 16 © Michael Cardinell/Extreme Wildlife Photography; p. 20 (inset) © Joe McDonald/CORBIS.

Manufactured in the United States of America

CONTENTS

RANGE OF COTTONMOUTHS

SWAMP SNAKES

Cottonmouths are poisonous snakes. A cottonmouth uses its mouth to frighten its enemies. When it believes that it is in danger, a cottonmouth curls its body into rings. Then it throws its head back and opens its mouth wide. It keeps its mouth open for as long as it feels that it is in danger, displaying its white, cottonlike mouth. This action gives the cottonmouth its name.

The three kinds of cottonmouths are Florida, eastern, and western. Most of them live in the southeastern United States. They live near swamps, rivers, shallow pools, and lakes. Cottonmouths are also called water moccasins. They swim as they hunt for **prey**.

This cottonmouth is swimming in the flooded Mississippi River. It is using the S-shaped movement, the same method of movement that it uses to move across the ground.

COLORED FOR CAMOUFLAGE

Cottonmouths are large snakes, about 48 inches (122 cm) in length. The record length for an adult cottonmouth is 74 ½ inches (189 cm). During its up to 20-year life span, a cottonmouth can grow to be as thick as a man's arm. Most cottonmouths are olive, tan, brown, or black in color. Most have dark rings around their bodies. Their bellies are yellow and sometimes have black or brown marks. Their coloring is called **camouflage**. It helps the snakes to blend with fallen leaves and branches, or plants in their surroundings. Then they can hunt for fish, frogs, lizards, birds, mice, small turtles, and even other snakes without being seen.

Top: A cottonmouth swims with its head and neck above water as it hunts for catfish. Bottom: Because cottonmouths, such as this eastern cottonmouth, live near swamps, they are dark in color.

SNAKEBITE
A COTTONMOUTH'S
SCIENTIFIC NAME IS
*AGKISTRODON
PISCIVORUS*. *PISCIVORUS*
MEANS "FISH EATING."

COLD-BLOODED CREATURES

Cottonmouths are **reptiles**. Reptiles have dry, scaly skin. They are also cold-blooded. This means that their body **temperature** changes with the temperature of their surroundings. Humans are warm-blooded. Their bodies generally keep an even temperature no matter what the temperature is around them. To warm up, cottonmouths lie in the sun. To cool down, they rest in the shade. In fall and spring, cottonmouths are usually active during the day. In the hot summer, they do most of their hunting at night. They **hibernate** in dens from late fall through winter. They come out of their dens in early spring, usually in March.

Cottonmouths, such as this one in Florida's Big Cypress National Preserve, have to move into the sun to warm up. The main source of body heat for all snakes comes from outside their bodies.

PIT VIPERS

Cottonmouths belong to the pit viper **family** of snakes. More than 290 **species** of pit vipers live around the world, including copperheads and rattlesnakes. These snakes have two pits, or holes, on their faces. Each pit is located between the snake's eye and its nostril. The pits contain heat-sensitive **membranes**. Cottonmouths rely on these pits to help them find prey and to help them escape from **predators**. Because the pits sense heat, a cottonmouth can find warm-blooded prey even in the dark, as long as the prey's body temperature is warmer than its surroundings.

A cottonmouth's pits, or heat sensors, are the holes that are located between the snake's eyes and nostrils.

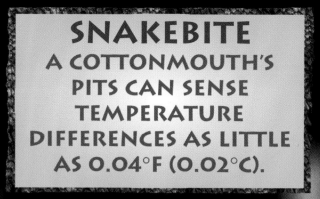

SNAKEBITE
A COTTONMOUTH'S PITS CAN SENSE TEMPERATURE DIFFERENCES AS LITTLE AS 0.04°F (0.02°C).

SNAKEBITE
TO MARK ITS AREA, A
COTTONMOUTH CAN
SPRAY A SMELLY
LIQUID, CALLED MUSK,
FROM NEAR ITS TAIL.

COTTONMOUTH SENSES

Cottonmouths rely on their pits and their senses of smell and taste to locate prey or predators. They have fork-shaped tongues, which give them more **surface area** to pick up traces of scents. They flick their tongues in and out of their mouths often to smell and to taste what is in the air, on the ground, and even in the water. Cottonmouths do not see faraway objects very well. They have better eyesight for objects that are close, except for when their eyes get covered with mud while digging for tadpoles! Snakes do not have eardrums. They hear animals and other moving things by feeling the **vibrations** made by movement.

Although it uses its nose to smell, this Florida cottonmouth also uses its tongue to pick up tiny traces of odor. A cottonmouth relies on its nose and tongue to help it smell and taste scents.

POWERFUL FANGS

Cottonmouths have a pair of movable teeth called **fangs**. A cottonmouth's fangs are hollow, and they fold back when the snake's mouth is closed. When a cottonmouth strikes, or bites, its fangs move forward. The powerful, hinged jaws of a cottonmouth enable it to hold on to prey until the **venom**, or poison, kills the prey. Venom **sacs** are located behind a cottonmouth's fangs. When the snake bites, the fangs pierce the prey's skin. The venom sacs are squeezed, and the venom is released into the prey through the hollow fangs. A cottonmouth can even bite prey while swimming in the water. It drags the **victim** to land before swallowing it whole.

Top: *A cottonmouth's curved fangs fold back into its mouth until the snake is ready to strike its prey.* Bottom: *This Florida cottonmouth digs a tadpole out of a mudhole.*

SNAKEBITE
COTTONMOUTHS CAUSE ONLY ABOUT 10 PERCENT OF THE 8,000 POISONOUS SNAKEBITES EACH YEAR IN THE UNITED STATES.

COTTONMOUTH VENOM

A cottonmouth's venom is very powerful. The amount of venom that a cottonmouth delivers in one bite is about $\frac{1}{200}$ ounce (142 mg). The amount of venom that can cause great harm or death to a human is about $\frac{1}{250}$ ounce (113 mg). Venom is a mixture of different **chemicals**. A pit viper has its own special mixture of chemicals. Cottonmouth venom is **hemotoxic**. It breaks down and destroys red blood cells and other tissues. For small animals, this venom is fatal. If a person is bitten, he or she should be treated immediately by a doctor. Without a doctor's help, that person could become sick or could die.

A scientist hooks a cottonmouth's fangs over the edge of a glass to take venom. This process is called milking a snake. The venom will be used to make antivenin, a medicine for treating snakebites.

Cottonmouths have several layers of skin. One layer gives the snake its pattern and coloring. Another layer grips the cottonmouth's scales. The scales protect a snake's body from harm. They also make it waterproof and keep the cottonmouth from drying out. Scales also help the snake to move on the ground or in the water. A cottonmouth's scales are keeled. This means that each scale has a ridge running down its center. Keeled scales make cottonmouths look dull so that they blend into their surroundings. As do all snakes, cottonmouths **molt**. They molt when their body grows or when the outer layer of skin becomes worn.

A keeled scale has a raised ridge running down its center. Keeled scales give cottonmouths, such as this Florida cottonmouth, a dull color pattern.

MATING AND BABY COTTONMOUTHS

Female and male cottonmouths **mate** every year, usually in the early spring. Male cottonmouths sometimes fight for the right to mate with a female. They can fight on land or in water. The female cottonmouth mates with the winner.

A female cottonmouth gives birth more than a year later, usually in August or September. She has live babies instead of laying eggs as some snakes do. She can give birth to as many as 16 babies. The babies are from 7 to 13 inches (18–33 cm) long. At birth, they have venom and already know how to hunt for prey, so they can take care of themselves.

Top: *Young Florida cottonmouths open their mouths as a warning.* Bottom: *A young cottonmouth uses its yellowish tail when hunting to trick prey into thinking the tail is a worm or a caterpillar.*

COTTONMOUTH ENEMIES

A cottonmouth's predators are king snakes, great blue herons, and largemouth bass. Humans are probably this snake's worst enemy. People are afraid that the snake will bite them, so they will kill a cottonmouth if they see one. Luckily for cottonmouths, they live in areas where people do not wish to live. Sadly, humans kill many harmless water snakes because they mistake them for cottonmouths. If you see a snake in the water with its head sticking out or one that opens its mouth wide, it is probably a cottonmouth. Any other snake is probably a water snake. A cottonmouth has venom and should be seen from afar!

GLOSSARY

camouflage (KA-muh-flaj) A pattern that matches its surroundings.

chemicals (KEH-mih-kulz) Matter that can be mixed with other matter to cause changes.

family (FAM-lee) The scientific name for a large group of plants or animals that are alike in some ways.

fangs (FANGZ) Sharp, hollow, or grooved teeth that inject venom.

hemotoxic (hee-muh-TOK-sik) Deadly to red blood cells and other tissues.

hibernate (HY-bur-nayt) To spend the winter sleeping or resting.

mate (MAYT) To join together to make babies.

membranes (MEM-braynz) Soft, thin layers of living matter that come from a plant or an animal.

molt (MOHLT) To shed hair, feathers, shell, horns, or skin.

predators (PREH-duh-terz) Animals that kill other animals for food.

prey (PRAY) An animal that is hunted by another animal for food.

reptiles (REP-tylz) Cold-blooded animals with lungs and scales.

sacs (SAKS) Pouchlike parts in a plant or animal.

species (SPEE-sheez) A single kind of plant or animal. All people are one species.

surface area (SER-fis AYR-ee-uh) The outside of something.

temperature (TEM-pruh-cher) The heat in a living body.

venom (VEH-num) A poison passed by one animal into another through a bite or sting. Venom helps snakes to catch and break down their prey as food.

vibrations (vy-BRAY-shunz) Fast movements up and down, or back and forth.

victim (VIK-tim) A person or an animal that is harmed or killed.

INDEX

WEB SITES

Due to the changing nature of Internet links, PowerKids Press has developed an online list of Web sites related to the subject of this book. This site is updated regularly. Please use this link to access the list:
www.powerkidslinks.com/rwls/cottonm/